# ITALIAN
# FOR BEGINNERS

### Angela Wilkes
### Illustrated by John Shackell

Designed by Roger Priddy
Edited by Nicole Irving
Language Consultants: Patrizia Di Bello & Giorgio Chiosso

## CONTENTS

Handlettering by Jack Potter

# About this book

Going abroad is much more fun if you can speak a little of the language. This book shows you that learning another language is a lot easier than you might think. It teaches you the Italian you will find useful in everyday situations.

## You can find out how to . . .

talk about yourself,

and your home,

count and tell the time,

say what you like,

find your way around

and ask for what you want in shops.

## How you learn

Picture strips like this show you what to say in each situation. Read the speech bubbles and see how much you can understand by yourself, then look up any words you do not know. Words and phrases are repeated again and again, to help you remember them.

The book starts with really easy things to say and gets more difficult towards the end.

## New words

All the new words you come across are listed on each double page, so you can look them up as you go along. If you forget any words you can look them up in the glossary on pages 46-48. *If you see an asterisk by a word, it means that there is a note about it at the bottom of the page.

## Grammar

Boxes like this around words show where new grammar is explained. You will find Italian easier if you learn some of its grammar, or rules, but don't worry if you don't understand it all straightaway. You can look up any of the grammar used in the book on pages 42-43.

## Internet links*

If you have access to a computer with an Internet connection, you can try out the Web sites described at the top of each double page. For links to these sites go to **www.usborne-quicklinks.com**

## Puzzles

Throughout the book there are puzzles and quizzes (with answers on pages 44-45). You'll find more puzzles that you can download for free at the Usborne Quicklinks Web site: **www.usborne-quicklinks.com**

## Practising your Italian

Write all the new words you learn in a notebook and try to learn a few every day. Keep going over them and you will soon remember them.

Ask a friend to keep testing you on your Italian. Even better, ask someone to learn Italian with you so that you can practise on each other.

Try to go to Italy for your holidays, and speak as much Italian as you can. Don't be afraid of making mistakes. No one will mind.

* For more information on using the Internet, see inside the front cover.

3

# Saying "Hello and Goodbye"

The first thing you should know how to say in Italian is "Hello". There are different greetings for different times of day. Here you can find out what to say when.

In Italy it is more polite to add **signora** or **signorina** when you greet a woman or a girl you don't know. The word for a man is **signore** but you don't often use it.

> Ciao, come stai?

> Non molto bene.

> Buonasera!

## Saying "Hello"

> Ciao Paolo!

This is how to say "Hello" to your friends.

> Buongiorno, signora.

> Buongiorno!

This is more polite and means "Have a good day".

> Buonasera!

This is how you say "Good evening" to someone.

## Saying "Goodbye"

> Ciao!

> Ciao!

**Ciao** can mean "Goodbye" as well as "Hello".

> Arrivederci!

> A presto.

These are different ways of saying "See you again".

## Saying "Goodnight"

> Buona notte!

You only say **Buona notte** last thing at night.

4

## How are you?

This is how to greet someone and ask how they are.

This person is saying that she is fine, thank you...

...but this one is saying things aren't too good.

## Come stai?

This list shows you different ways of saying how you are, from very well to terrible. What do you think each of the people here would say if you asked them how they were?

| | |
|---|---|
| **molto bene** | very well |
| **bene** | well |
| **benino** | quite well |
| **non molto bene** | not very well |
| **molto male** | terrible |

5

# What is your name?

Here you can find out how to ask someone their name and tell them yours, and how to introduce your friends. Read the picture strip and see how much you can understand. Then try doing the puzzles on the page opposite.

## New words

| | |
|---|---|
| io* | I |
| tu* | you |
| lui* | he |
| lei* | she |
| loro* | they |
| come ti chiami (tu)? | what are you called? |
| come si chiama (lui/lei)? | what is he/she called? |
| come si chiamano (loro)? | what are they called? |
| io mi chiamo | I am called |
| lui si chiama | he is called |
| lei si chiama | she is called |
| loro si chiamano | they are called |
| chi è lui/lei? | who is he/she? |
| chi è quello /quella? | who is that? (male/female) |
| questo/questa è | this is (m/f) |
| il mio amico | my friend (m) |
| la mia amica | my friend (f) |
| e tu? | and you? |
| sì | yes |
| no | no |

## Chi è?

In Italian to ask "who is that?", "who is he/she?", "who is it?" or even "who is who?" you can simply ask **chi è?**

Buongiorno, come ti chiami?

Dario, e tu?

Io mi chiamo Monica.

**Introducing friends**

Questo è un mio amico. Si chiama Piero.

Chi è lei?

Lei è una mia amica. Si chiama Maria.

Come si chiamano?

Loro si chiamano Paolo e Gianni.

*In Italian these words are often left out.

## What are they called?

Can you answer these questions in Italian?

Come si chiama la mia amica ?

E tu, come ti chiami ?

Come si chiama?

Come si chiamano?

## Who is who?

Can you answer the questions below the picture?

Ciao, come stai ?

Sto bene, grazie.

Arrivederci, Nicola.

Quella è Anna ?

Si, quella è Anna.

Arrivederci!

È Gianni.

Chi è quello?

No, io mi chiamo Michele.

Tu ti chiami Dario ?

Come ti chiami ?

Valeria, e tu ?

Who is talking to Gianni?
Who is talking to Valeria?

Who is called Michele?
Who is talking to him?

Who is called Anna?
Who is going home?

## Can you remember?

How would you ask someone their name?
How would you tell them your name?

You have a friend called Valeria. How would you introduce her to someone?
How would you tell someone your friend is called Daniele?

# Finding out what things are called

Everything on this picture has its name on it. See if you can learn the names for everything, then try the memory test at the bottom of the opposite page. You can find out what **il**, **lo**, **l'** and **la** mean in the box below the picture.

il comignolo

il tetto

il sole

l' uccello

il nido

l' albero

la finestra

il fiore

*Buon-giorno!*

la casa

*Questa è la mia casa.*

la porta

il garage

lo steccato

il cane

il gatto

la macchina

## Il, lo, l' and la words

Italian nouns are masculine or feminine. The word for "the" shows the gender: **Il** (or **lo**) before masculine (m) nouns, **la** before feminine (f) ones and **l'** before all nouns starting with a vowel.* "A" or "an" is **un** before **il** and masculine **l'** words (**uno** before **lo** words), **una** before **la** words, **un'** before feminine **l'** words.

| | | | | | |
|---|---|---|---|---|---|
| **il sole** | sun | **il garage** | garage | **lo steccato** | fence |
| **il tetto** | roof | **il fiore** | flower | **la casa** | house |
| **il gatto** | cat | **il comignolo** | chimney | **la finestra** | window |
| **il cane** | dog | **l' albero (m)** | tree | **la porta** | door |
| **il nido** | nest | **l' uccello (m)** | bird | **la macchina** | car |

*Always learn which word to use with each noun.

## Asking what things are called

Don't worry if you don't know what something is called in Italian. To find out what it is, just ask someone **che cos'è?** Look at the list of useful phrases below, then read the picture strip to see how to use them.

| | |
|---|---|
| **che cos'è?** | what is it? |
| **questo è . . .** | this is . . . (m) |
| **questa è . . .** | this is . . . (f) |
| **anche** | also |
| **in italiano** | in Italian |
| **in inglese** | in English |

Che cos'è ?

Un fiore.

Anche questo è un fiore ?

No, questo è un albero.

Che cos'è in italiano?

Questa è una porta.

E questo cos'è ?

Questo è un cane.

Che cos'è in inglese?

A dog !

## Can you remember?

Cover up the opposite page and see if you can name these things in Italian. Don't forget to say whether they are **il**, **lo**, **l'** or **la** words.

9

# Where do you come from?

Here you can find out how to ask people where they come from. You can also find out how to ask if they speak Italian.

## New words

| | |
|---|---|
| da* dove vieni? | where do you come from? |
| io vengo da . . . | I come from . . . |
| dove abiti? | where do you live? |
| io abito a . . . | I live in (town) |
| io abito in . . . | I live in (country) |
| tu parli . . ? | do you speak . . ? |
| io parlo | I speak . . . |
| un poco | a little |
| italiano | Italian |
| inglese | English |
| tedesco | German |
| ecco | here is |
| noi | we |
| voi | you (plural) |

## Countries

| | |
|---|---|
| l'Italia (f) | Italy |
| la Germania | Germany |
| l' Inghilterra (f) | England |
| la Francia | France |
| l' India (f) | India |
| la Scozia | Scotland |
| l' Austria (f) | Austria |
| la Spagna | Spain |
| l' Ungheria (f) | Hungary |

## Where do you come from?

## Do you speak Italian?

10   *Da means "from". Dalla means "from the" (feminine); it changes to dall' before a feminine word beginning with a vowel: Io vengo dall' Inghilterra (I come from England).

## Who comes from where?

These are the contestants for an international dancing competition. They have come from all over the world. The compère does not speak any Italian and does not understand where anyone comes from. Read about the contestants, then see if you can tell him what he wants to know. His questions are beneath the picture.

*Angus viene dalla Scozia.*

*Ecco Marie e Pierre. Loro vengono dalla Francia.*

*Hari e Indira vengono dall' India.*

*Yuri viene dall' Ungheria. Abita a Budapest.*

*Franz viene dall' Austria.*

*Ecco Lolita. Lei viene dalla Spagna.*

Where do they all come from?

Where does Franz come from?
What are the Indian contestants called?
Is Lolita Italian or Spanish?

Is there a Scottish contestant?
Where do Marie and Pierre come from?
Who lives in Budapest? Where is Budapest?

| **Verbs (action words)** | **parlare** | to speak | **venire** | to come |
|---|---|---|---|---|
| Italian verbs change according to who is doing the action. Verbs ending in **are** follow the same pattern and have the same endings as **parlare**. You will have to learn **venire** by itself.* | **io parlo** | I speak | **io vengo** | I come |
| | **tu parli** | you speak | **tu vieni** | you come |
| | **lui/lei parla** | he/she speaks | **lui/lei viene** | he/she comes |
| | **noi parliamo** | we speak | **noi veniamo** | we come |
| | **voi parlate** | you speak (pl) | **voi venite** | you come (pl) |
| | **loro parlano** | they speak | **loro vengono** | they come |

### Can you remember?

How would you ask someone where they come from?

Can you say where you come from?
How do you say that you speak Italian?
How would you ask someone if they can?

# More about you

Here you can find out how to count up to 20, say how old you are and say how many brothers and sisters you have.

To say how old you are in Italian, you say how many years you have. So if you are ten, you say **io ho dieci anni** (I have ten years).

## New words

| | |
|---|---|
| **quanti anni hai?** | How old are you? |
| **io ho cinque anni** | I am five years old |
| **tu hai . . ?** | have you . . ? |
| **io ho** | I have |
| **io non ho** | I have no |
| **nessun(o) /nessuna** | not any |
| **il fratello** | brother |
| **la sorella** | sister |
| **quasi** | almost |
| **né** | nor |
| **ma** | but |

## Plural words

Italian nouns and the word for "the" change when you are talking about more than one thing. Masculine words: **il** becomes **i**, **lo** and **l'** become **gli**, and the final letter changes to **i**. Feminine words: **la** and **l'** become **le**, and the final **letter** changes to **e**.*

## Numbers**

| | | | |
|---|---|---|---|
| 1 | uno | 11 | undici |
| 2 | due | 12 | dodici |
| 3 | tre | 13 | tredici |
| 4 | quattro | 14 | quattordici |
| 5 | cinque | 15 | quindici |
| 6 | sei | 16 | sedici |
| 7 | sette | 17 | diciassette |
| 8 | otto | 18 | diciotto |
| 9 | nove | 19 | diciannove |
| 10 | dieci | 20 | venti |

## How old are you?

## Have you any brothers and sisters?

12      *You can read about plurals on pages 42-43.      **You will find a complete list of numbers on page 40.

## How old are they?

Read what these children are saying, then see if you can say how old they all are.

Giulio ha dodici anni.

Noi abbiamo quindici anni.

Paola ha undici anni.

Michele ha quasi quattordici anni.

Io ho cinque anni. Lui ha nove anni.

Michele        Diana e Silvia        Giulio        Paola        Luca        Lisa

## How many brothers and sisters?

Below you can read how many brothers and sisters the children have. Can you work out who has which brothers and sisters?

Diana e Silvia hanno un fratello e due sorelle.

Paola ha tre sorelle e due fratelli.

Michele ha cinque sorelle, ma nessun fratello.

Luca ha un fratello, ma nessuna sorella.

Giulio non ha fratelli né sorelle, ma ha un cane.

## Useful verbs

| **avere** | to have |
|---|---|
| **io ho** | I have |
| **tu hai** | you have |
| **lui/lei ha** | he/she/it has |
| **noi abbiamo** | we have |
| **voi avete** | you have (pl) |
| **loro hanno** | they have |

| **essere*** | to be |
|---|---|
| **io sono** | I am |
| **tu sei** | you are |
| **lui/lei è** | he/she/it is |
| **noi siamo** | we are |
| **voi siete** | you are (pl) |
| **loro sono** | they are |

*__Essere__ is used on the next page, so it may help you to learn it now.

# Talking about your family

On these two pages you will learn lots of words which help you to talk about your family. You will also find out how to say "my" and "your" and describe people.

Ecco la mia famiglia.

il mio cane

mio nonno

mio padre

mia sorella

mio zio

il mio gatto

mia nonna

mia madre

mio fratello

mia zia

## Who's who?

Questo è tuo fratello?

Sì, è mio fratello.

E questa, è tua sorella?

Sì, si chiama Ilaria.

Sono i tuoi genitori?

No! Sono i miei nonni.

## New words

| | | | | | |
|---|---|---|---|---|---|
| **la famiglia** | family | **la zia** | aunt | **magro/magra** | thin |
| **il nonno** | grandfather | **i nonni** | grandparents | **vecchio/vecchia** | old |
| **la nonna** | grandmother | **i genitori** | parents | **giovane (m and f)** | young |
| **il padre** | father | **alto/alta** | tall | **biondo/bionda** | blond |
| **la madre** | mother | **basso/bassa** | small/short | **castano/castana** | chestnut brown |
| **lo zio** | uncle | **grasso/grassa** | fat | **affettuoso/a** | friendly |

## How to say "my" and "your"

When you say "my" or "your" in Italian, you don't usually drop the word for "the", e.g. **la mia famiglia** (my family).

"My" and "your" also change depending on whether you are talking about a masculine, feminine or plural word.*

| | my | your |
|---|---|---|
| il words | **(il) mio**\*\* | **(il) tuo**\*\* |
| la words | **(la) mia** | **(la) tua** |
| i plurals | **(i) miei** | **(i) tuoi** |
| le plurals | **(le) mie** | **(le) tue** |

14   *You can find out more about this on pages 42-43.
    \*\*Before **mio** and **tuo** you use **il**, even if it is a **lo** word, e.g. **lo steccato**, **il mio steccato** (the fence, my fence).

## Describing your family

*Mio padre è alto e mia madre è bassa.*

*Mia madre è alta e mio padre è basso.*

*Mio zio è grasso e mia zia è magra.*

*I miei nonni sono vecchi. Io sono giovane.*

*Mia sorella è bionda. Mio fratello è castano.*

*Il mio cane è affettuoso.*

## Describing words

Italian adjectives change their endings depending on whether they are describing a masculine or feminine word. In the word list both forms are shown. Usually the **o** at the end of the masculine form changes to **a** in the feminine, e.g. **alto, alta.**\*

Can you describe each of these people in Italian, starting **Lui è …** or **Lei è…?**

*You can find out more about adjectives on pages 42-43.

15

# Your home

Here you can find out how to say what sort of home you live in and whereabouts it is. You can also learn what all the rooms are called.

## New words

| | |
|---|---|
| **o** | or |
| **la casa** | house |
| **l'appartamento (m)** | flat |
| **il castello** | castle |
| **in città\*** | in the town |
| **in campagna** | in the country |
| **in riva al mare** | by the sea |
| **babbo (or papà)** | Dad |
| **mamma** | Mum |
| **nonno** | Grandad |
| **nonna** | Granny |
| **il fantasma** | ghost |
| **dove siete?** | where are you? (pl) |
| **il bagno** | bathroom |
| **la stanza da pranzo** | dining room |
| **la stanza da letto** | bedroom |
| **il soggiorno** | living room |
| **la cucina** | kitchen |
| **l' ingresso (m)** | hall |
| **il piano di sopra** | upstairs |

## Where do you live?

Tu abiti in una casa o in un appartamento?

Io abito in una casa.

Io abito in un appartamento.

Io abito in un castello.

## Town or country?

Io abito in città.

Io abito in campagna.

Io abito in riva al mare.

16  \***In** means "in". It becomes **nel**, **nello** before **il**, **lo** words; **nella** before **la** words; **nell'** before **l'** words.

## Where is everyone?

Babbo comes home and wants to know where everyone is. Look at the pictures and see if you can tell him where everyone is, e.g. **Nonna è** **nel soggiorno**. Then see if you can answer the questions below the little pictures.

mamma  babbo  nonno

nonna  Piero  Isabella

Simone  il fantasma

Chi è nella stanza da pranzo?
Chi è in cucina?
Chi è in bagno?
Chi è nella stanza da letto?

Dov'è mamma?
Dov'è il fantasma?
Dov'è il cane?
Dov'è Piero?
Dov'è babbo? (Look at the word list)

## Can you remember?

How do you ask someone where they live?
How do you ask whether they live in a house or a flat?

Can you remember how to say "in the country"?
Can you remember how to say "in the town"?

How would you tell someone you were upstairs?
How would you tell them you were in the kitchen?

17

# Looking for things

Here you can find out how to ask someone what they are looking for and tell them where things are. You can also learn lots of words for things around the house.

## New words

| | |
|---|---|
| cercare | to look for |
| qualcosa | something |
| il criceto | hamster |
| trovare | to find |
| lo | him/it |
| sopra | on |
| sotto | under |
| dietro | behind |
| davanti a | in front of |
| tra | between |
| a fianco a | next to |
| il mobile | cupboard |
| l' armadio (m) | wardrobe |
| la poltrona | armchair |
| la tenda | curtain |
| la pianta | plant |
| lo scaffale | shelf |
| la tavola | table |
| il tappeto | carpet |
| il divano | sofa |
| la televisione | television |
| il telefono | telephone |
| il vaso | vase |
| eccolo! | there it/he is! |

## He, she, it

When you are talking about things in Italian, the verb alone makes clear what you are talking about, and you don't use any word for "it":

Dov'è il telefono?
**È sulla tavola.**

It is the same when you are talking about people or pets: although there are words for "he" and "she" – **lui** and **lei**, you usually use the verb on its own.

## The missing hamster

Cerchi qualcosa?

Cerco il mio criceto. Non lo trovo!

Non è sopra l'armadio.

Non è sotto il divano.

È dietro la tenda?

No.

Eccolo! Tra le piante!

18

## In, on or under?

Try to learn these words by heart. With **davanti al**, **a fianco al**, **al** changes to **allo** before a **lo** word, **alla** before a **la** word and **all'** before a word beginning with a vowel.

*dentro*  *dietro*  *davanti a*  *a fianco a*  *sotto*  *sopra*

## Where are they hiding?

Signor Bianchi's six pets are hiding somewhere in the room, but he cannot find them. Can you tell him where they are in Italian, using the words above?

*il criceto*

*il gatto*

*il cane*

*il pappagallo*

*il serpente*

*la tartaruga*

lo scaffale

il vaso

il mobile

la televisione

il telefono

il tappeto

la tavola

la poltrona

il divano

# What do you like eating?

Here you can find out how to say what you like and don't like.

## New words

| | |
|---|---|
| mi piace | I like |
| ti piace? | do you like? |
| non mi piace* | I don't like |
| cosa . . ? | what . . ? |
| amare | to love |
| non . . . affatto | not at all |
| allora | then |
| molto | a lot |
| di più | more/the most |
| io preferisco | I prefer |
| soprattutto | above all |
| l' insalata (f) | salad |
| il pesce | fish |
| le patate fritte | chips |
| la torta | cake |
| le salsicce | sausages |
| gli spaghetti | spaghetti |
| mangiare | to eat |
| la pizza | pizza |
| l' amburgher (m) | hamburger |
| il riso | rice |
| il pane | bread |
| il formaggio | cheese |
| anche a me | (to) me too |

## What do you like?

Ti piace l'insalata?

No, non mi piace l'insalata.

Ti piace il pesce?

No, non mi piace affatto.

Cosa ti piace, allora?

Mi piacciono le patate fritte.

E amo le torte!

## What do you like best?

Cosa ti piace di più?

Mi piacciono molto le salsicce.

. . . Ma preferisco la pizza.

. . . E soprattutto amo molto gli spaghetti!

*You can read more about negatives on pages 42-43.

*Internet link:* a quiz game for one or two people about eating and drinking.
For a hundred points, can you type in the correct Italian word?
Go to **www.usborne-quicklinks.com** for a link to this site.

# What are they eating?

Cosa mangi?

Io mangio una pizza.

Lei mangia delle * patate fritte.

Lui mangia del pane e formaggio.

Noi mangiamo degli amburgher.

Voi mangiate del riso.

Loro mangiano delle banane.

## Who likes what?

Who likes cheese? Who doesn't like ham? Who prefers grapes to bananas?

Can you say in Italian which things you like and which you don't like?

Anche a me, ma non mi piace il prosciutto.

Gianni

Mi piacciono le banane.

Simone

Io preferisco l'uva.

nonno

Mi piace il formaggio.

Diego

Mi piace soprattutto la crostata di frutta.

Isabella

il prosciutto   il burro   la pizza

il pane

l'insalata   i pomodori   il formaggio

le banane   l'uva   una crostata di frutta   il succo d'arancia

---

**Mi piace, mi piacciono**

Where in English we say "I like", the Italians say "(it) pleases me": **mi piace** or

"(they) please me": **mi piacciono**.

| | |
|---|---|
| **mi piace/piacciono** | I like |
| **ti piace/piacciono** | you like |

---

*\*Del, dello* etc. can mean "some", so **Lei mangia delle patate fritte** means "She is eating some chips". You can read more about this on page 42.

21

# Table talk

Here you can learn all sorts of useful things to say if you are having a meal with Italian friends.

## New words

| | |
|---|---|
| **a tavola, è pronto** | come to the table, it's ready |
| **ho fame** | I am hungry |
| **anche io** | me too |
| **serviti** | help yourself |
| **servitevi** | help yourselves |
| **buon appetito** | enjoy the meal |
| **grazie, altrettanto** | thank you, and you too |
| **mi puoi passare . . .** | can you pass me . . . |
| **l' acqua (f)** | water |
| **il pane** | bread |
| **il bicchiere** | glass |
| **lei vuole . . ?*** | would you like . . ? |
| **ancora** | more |
| **la carne** | meat |
| **sì, grazie** | yes, please |
| **no, grazie** | no, thanks |
| **è abbastanza** | I've had enough |
| **è buono?** | is it good? |
| **è delizioso** | it's delicious |

## Dinner is ready

A tavola, è pronto!

Ho fame.

Anche io!

Prego, serviti!

Grazie.

Buon appetito!

Grazie, altrettanto!

## Please will you pass me . . .

Mi puoi passare l'acqua, per favore?

Mi puoi passare il pane, per favore?

Mi puoi passare un bicchiere, per favore?

*Lei is a polite way of saying "you". You can find out more about it on page 23.

*Internet link:* select the BBC "Eating Out" challenge. Can you take your Italian friend's family out for a meal, without speaking a word of English? Go to **www.usborne-quicklinks.com** for a link to this site.

## Would you like some more?

> Lei vuole ancora carne?

> Si, grazie.

> Vuole ancora patate fritte?

> No, grazie. È abbastanza.

> È buono?

> Sì, è delizioso.

## Who is saying what?

These little pictures show you different things that can happen at mealtime.

Cover up the rest of the page and see if you can say what everyone would say in Italian.

Simone is saying he is hungry.

The chef wants you to enjoy your meal.

Isabella is saying "Help yourself".

Piero wants someone to pass him a glass.

Nonna is offering Simone more chips.

He says "Yes please" and that he likes chips.

Then he says "No thanks. That's enough."

Marco is saying the food is delicious.

## Lei

**Lei** is used as a polite way of saying "you", for example to somebody you don't know. With **lei**, the verb follows the "she" form (whether you are talking to a man or a woman), e.g. **Signore, lei vuole ancora carne? Signora, lei vuole ancora patate fritte?**

23

# Your hobbies

These people are talking about their hobbies.

## New words

| | |
|---|---|
| fare | to do/make |
| dipingere | to paint |
| cucinare | to cook |
| tempo libero | spare time |
| fare del modellismo | to build models |
| ballare | to dance |
| leggere | to read |
| guardare la televisione | to watch TV |
| lavorare a maglia | to knit |
| nuotare | to swim |
| giocare | to play |
| lo sport | sport |
| il calcio | football |
| il tennis | tennis |
| la musica | music |
| ascoltare | to listen to |
| suonare | to play (music) |
| lo strumento | instrument |
| il violino | violin |
| il pianoforte | piano |
| di sera | in the evening |

### fare (to make or do)

| | |
|---|---|
| io faccio | I do |
| tu fai | you do |
| lui/lei fa | he/she does |
| noi facciamo | we do |
| voi fate | you do (pl) |
| loro fanno | they do |

### giocare and suonare

When you talk about playing a sport or a game, you say **giocare a**, then the name of the sport, e.g. **gioco a calcio**. (I play football).

To talk about playing an instrument, you say **suonare**, e.g. **suono il pianoforte** (I play the piano).

## What do you do in the evenings?

24

## The sporty type

Cosa fai nel tempo libero?

Io amo lo sport!

Nuoto,

gioco a calcio

e io gioco a tennis.

## Music lovers

Voi cosa fate nel tempo libero?

Noi amiamo ascoltare la musica.

Suonate degli* strumenti?

E io suono il pianoforte.

Sì, io suono il violino.

## What are they doing?

A

B

C

D

E

Cover up the rest of the page and see if you can say what all these people are doing in

Italian, e.g. **Lui gioca a calcio.**
What are your hobbies?

*Degli here means "any". You can read more about this on pages 42-43.

# Telling the time

Here you can find out how to tell the time in Italian. You can look up any numbers you don't know on page 40.

There is no word for "past" in Italian. To say "past five" you say **e cinque** (and five); to say "five to" you say **meno cinque** (minus five), after the hour: **sono le nove meno cinque** (it is five to nine).

## What is the time?

Here is how to ask what the time is.

## New words

| | |
|---|---|
| **che ore sono?** | what is the time? |
| **è l'una** | it is one o'clock |
| **sono le due** | it is two o'clock |
| **meno cinque** | five to |
| **e un quarto** | quarter past |
| **meno un quarto** | quarter to |
| **e mezza*** | half past |
| **mezzanotte** | midnight |
| **mezzogiorno** | midday |
| **del mattino** | in the morning |
| **della sera** | in the evening |
| **all' una** | at one |
| **alle due** | at two |
| **alzarsi** | to get up |
| **fare colazione** | to have breakfast |
| **il pranzo** | lunch |
| **la cena** | supper, dinner |
| **lui va** | he goes |
| **a scuola** | to school |
| **a letto** | to bed |

## andare (to go)

| | |
|---|---|
| **io vado** | I go |
| **tu vai** | you go |
| **lui/lei va** | he/she goes |
| **noi andiamo** | we go |
| **voi andate** | you go (pl) |
| **loro vanno** | they go |

## The time is . . .

Sono le nove e cinque.

Sono le nove e un quarto.

Sono le nove e mezza.

Sono le dieci meno un quarto.

Sono le dieci meno cinque.

È mezzogiorno/ mezzanotte.

## What time of day?

Sono le sei del mattino.

Sono le sei della sera.

26   *To say "half past twelve" you say **mezzanotte/mezzogiorno e mezza.**

## Marco's day

Read what Marco does throughout the day, then see if you can match each clock with the right picture. You can find out what the answers are on pages 44-45.

 a
 b
 c
 d
 e
 f
 g
 h

**1**
Marco si alza alle sette e mezza.*

**2**
Fa colazione alle otto.

**3**
Alle nove meno un quarto va a scuola.

**4**
Mangia il pranzo a mezzogiorno e mezza.

**5**
Alle due e dieci gioca a calcio.

**6**
Alle cinque e un quarto guarda la televisione.

**7**
Mangia la cena alle sei.

**8**
E va a letto alle otto e mezza.

## What time is it?

Can you say in Italian what times these clocks show?

*Some verbs are formed from two parts. You can read about these on pages 42-43.

27

# Arranging things

Here is how to arrange
things with your friends.

## New words

| | |
|---|---|
| **andiamo . . ?** | shall we go . . ? |
| **quando?** | when? |
| **martedì** | Tuesday |
| **di mattina** | in the morning |
| **di pomeriggio** | in the afternoon |
| **di sera** | in the evening |
| **la piscina** | swimming pool |
| **verso** | at about |
| **a martedì** | until Tuesday |
| **oggi** | today |
| **ci vediamo** | see you |
| **domani** | tomorrow |
| **stasera** | this evening |
| **va bene** | O.K. |
| **non posso** | I can't |
| **che peccato!** | what a pity! |
| **andare a /in** | to go to |
| **il cinema** | cinema |
| **la festa** | party |

## Days of the week

| | |
|---|---|
| **la domenica** | Sunday |
| **il lunedì** | Monday |
| **il martedì** | Tuesday |
| **il mercoledì** | Wednesday |
| **il giovedì** | Thursday |
| **il venerdì** | Friday |
| **il sabato** | Saturday |

## Tennis

## Swimming

## Going to the cinema

28

*Internet link:* watch a BBC video clip of people making arrangements over the phone - the transcript will help. Go to **www.usborne-quicklinks.com** for a link to this site.

## Going to a party

## Your diary for the week

Here is your diary, showing you what you are doing for a week. Read it, then see if you can answer the questions at the bottom of the page in Italian.

Che cosa fai venerdì?
Quando giochi a tennis?
Quando vai al cinema?
Quando suoni il pianoforte?
Che cosa fai domenica?*
A che ora è la festa, sabato?**

**a**
A means to, at: **al cinema** (to/at the cinema), **alle otto** (at eight). It becomes **al, allo** before **il, lo** words; **alla** before **la** words, **all'** before **l'** words; **ai, agli** before **i, gli** words; **alle** before **le** words (see also page 19).

*Che cosa?/Cosa? What? **A che ora? At what time?

# Asking where places are

Here and on the next two pages you can find out how to ask your way around.

Remember, in Italian there are two words for "you" -**tu** and **lei**. You say **tu** to a friend, but it is more polite to say **lei** when you are talking to an adult you don't know well.*

## New words

| | |
|---|---|
| scusi | excuse me |
| prego | not at all |
| qui | here |
| là/lì | over there |
| la posta | post office |
| nella piazza del mercato | in the market place |
| l' albergo (m) | hotel |
| poi | then |
| giri . . . | turn . . . |
| vada . . . | go . . . |
| c'è . . ? | is there . . ? |
| qui vicino | nearby |
| la via, la strada | street, road |
| è lontano? | is it far? |
| solo | only |
| proprio | just |
| a piedi | on foot |
| il supermercato | supermarket |
| di fronte a . . . | opposite . . . |
| la banca | bank |
| la farmacia | chemist's |

## Being polite

> Scusi . . .

> Grazie.

> Prego.

This is how to say "Excuse me . . . "

When people thank you, it is polite to answer "**Prego**".

## Where is . . ?

> Scusi signora, dov'è la posta?

> Lì, proprio a fianco al supermercato.

> Dov'è l'albergo della stazione, per favore?

> Giri qui a sinistra, poi vada diritto.

### Directions

diritto

a sinistra   a destra

*You can read more about this on page 23.

*Internet link:* explore the fascinating regions of Italy and discover more about their geography and culture. Go to **www.usborne-quicklinks.com** for a link to this site.

## Is there a … nearby?

## Is it far?

## Other useful places to ask for

| | | | |
|---|---|---|---|
| la stazione | una stazione di servizio | i gabinetti | una buca delle lettere |
| the station | a petrol station | toilets | a letter box |
| una cabina telefonica | un campeggio | l'ospedale | l'aeroporto |
| a telephone box | a campsite | the hospital | the airport |

# Finding your way around

Here you can find out how to ask your way around and follow directions. When you have read everything, try the map puzzle on the opposite page.

> Scusi, come si va alla stazione?

> Prenda la prima a destra, poi la seconda a sinistra.

> La stazione è sulla destra. *

> Come si va all'albergo della gioventù, per favore?

> Vada diritto fino alla stazione...

> Poi prenda la terza strada a destra.

> Come si va all' ufficio del turismo, per favore?

> In macchina? Continui diritto...

> Poi prenda la prima strada a sinistra.

*Sulla destra, sulla sinistra: on the right, on the left.

*Internet link:* follow Giovanna on her way to an art gallery, and Ricardo and Giuseppe on their way to the coast. Go to **www.usborne-quicklinks.com** for a link to this site.

## New words

| | | | |
|---|---|---|---|
| **come si va?** | how does one get to? | **fino a . . .** | as far as . . . |
| **prenda . . .** | take . . . | **in macchina** | by car |
| **continui . . .** | carry on . . . | **la prima strada** | the first road |
| **l'albergo (m)** | youth hostel | **la seconda** | the second |
| **della gioventù** | | **la terza** | the third |
| **l'ufficio (m)** | tourist office | **il Municipio** | town hall |
| **del turismo** | | **la chiesa** | church |

| **prendere** | to take | | | When people are telling you |
|---|---|---|---|---|
| **io prendo** | I take | **noi prendiamo** | we take | where to go, to be more |
| **tu prendi** | you take | **voi prendete** | you take (pl) | polite they say **prenda** e.g. |
| **lui/lei prende** | he/she takes | **loro prendono** | they take | **Prenda la prima a destra.** |

## Finding your way around Città di Castello

How would you ask someone the way to the market place? How would you ask them if there is a café nearby? Ask how far it is.

Can you tell the person in the yellow car how to get to the church?
Can you direct someone from the hotel to the market?

Where would these directions take the yellow car?
**Prenda la seconda via a sinistra, poi è sulla destra.**

# Going shopping

Here and on the next two pages you can find out how to say what you want when you go shopping. When you go into an Italian shop you should say "**Buongiorno**" (during the day) or "**Buonasera**" (in the evening).

## Italian money

One **Lira** is worth so little that the smallest coin is **Cinque Lire** or **L.5**. You need to remember **Cento Lire** (**L.100**) and **Mille Lire** (**L.1000**). To understand prices you must know the numbers in Italian. They are listed on page 40.

## New words

| | |
|---|---|
| fare la spesa | to go shopping |
| comprare | to buy |
| il panettiere | the baker |
| il negozio di alimentari | the grocer |
| il macellaio | the butcher |
| il latte | milk |
| l'uovo (m), le uova (f) | egg, eggs |
| la frutta | fruit |
| la verdura | vegetables |
| la carne | meat |
| il panino | bread roll |
| la mela | apple |
| il pomodoro | tomato |
| desidera? | can I help you? |
| vorrei . . . | I would like . . . |
| sì, certo | yes, certainly |
| basta così? | is that all? |
| nient'altro? | anything else? |
| quant'è /quanto costa? | how much is it? |
| ecco | there you are |
| un litro | a litre |
| un chilo (Kg) | a kilo |
| mezzo chilo | half a kilo |
| allora | so, well then |

## Signora Bonomi goes shopping

La signora Bonomi va a fare la spesa.

Compra il pane dal panettiere.

## Dal panettiere

Buon-giorno!

Buongiorno signora, desidera?

Vorrei quattro panini.

Sì certo. Basta così?

Seicento Lire, per favore.

Sì grazie. Quant'è?

Ecco! Grazie.

*Internet link:* try to memorize the names of vegetables then move to the next page to see how much you remember. Go to **www.usborne-quicklinks.com** for a link to this site.

Compra il latte e le uova al negozio di alimentari.

Compra la frutta e la verdura al mercato.

Compra la carne dal macellaio.

## Dagli alimentari

## Al mercato

Desidera?

Sei uova per favore.

Nient'altro, signora?

Sì, un litro di latte, per favore.

Quant'è?

Allora sono mille Lire.

L.1000

Buongiorno signora.

Un chilo di mele per favore.

Altro?

Mezzo chilo di pomodori.

Sono mille e cinquecento Lire, per favore.

L.1500

# More shopping and going to a café

Here you can find out how to ask how much things cost and how to order things in a café.

## Asking how much things cost

Quanto costa questa cartolina?

Duecento Lire.

Quanto costa quell'uva?

Mille e trecento al chilo.

L.1300

## New words

| | |
|---|---|
| costare | to cost |
| quanto costa /costano? | how much is /are? |
| la cartolina | postcard |
| l'uva (f) | grapes |
| al chilo | . . . a kilo |
| l'uno/l'una | each (m/f) |
| la rosa | rose |
| me ne dà sette | give me seven |
| il caffè | coffee |
| il bar | café |
| il conto | bill |
| l'arancia (f) | orange |
| la banana | banana |
| l'ananas (m) | pineapple |
| il limone | lemon |
| la pesca | peach |
| la gazzosa | lemonade |
| la coca-cola | coca-cola |
| il tè | tea |
| con latte | with milk |
| un tè al limone | lemon tea |
| una cioccolata | hot chocolate |
| un bicchiere di . . . | a glass of . . . |
| un gelato | ice-cream |

Quanto costano le rose?

Settecento-cinquanta l'una.

L.750

Allora me ne dà sette.

---

## Going to a café

Desidera?

Un caffè, per favore.

Ecco!

Grazie.

Il conto per favore.

Sono mille e cinquecento Lire.

## Buying fruit

Everything on the fruit stall is marked with its name and price.

Look at the picture, then see if you can answer the questions below it.

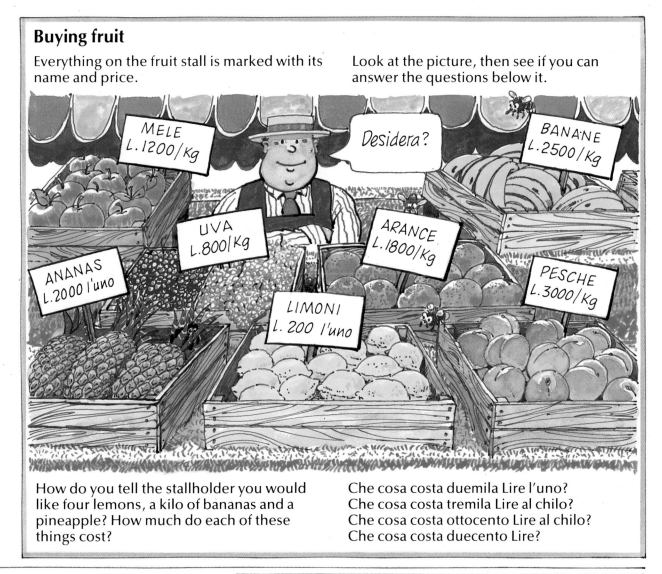

How do you tell the stallholder you would like four lemons, a kilo of bananas and a pineapple? How much do each of these things cost?

Che cosa costa duemila Lire l'uno?
Che cosa costa tremila Lire al chilo?
Che cosa costa ottocento Lire al chilo?
Che cosa costa duecento Lire?

## Things to order

Here are some things you might want to order in a café.

Vorrei...

| una gazzosa | una coca-cola | un tè con latte | un tè al limone |
| --- | --- | --- | --- |
| un succo d'arancia | una cioccolata | un bicchiere di latte | un gelato |

37

# The months and seasons

Here you can learn what the seasons and months are called and find out how to say what the date is.

## New words

| | |
|---|---|
| **il mese** | month |
| **l'anno (m)** | year |
| **quanti ne abbiamo?** | what is the date? |
| **oggi** | today |
| **il compleanno** | birthday |

## The seasons

| | |
|---|---|
| **la primavera** | spring |
| **l'estate (f)** | summer |
| **l'autunno (m)** | autumn |
| **l'inverno (m)** | winter |

## The months

| | |
|---|---|
| **gennaio** | January |
| **febbraio** | February |
| **marzo** | March |
| **aprile** | April |
| **maggio** | May |
| **giugno** | June |
| **luglio** | July |
| **agosto** | August |
| **settembre** | September |
| **ottobre** | October |
| **novembre** | November |
| **dicembre** | December |

## The seasons

*la primavera*

*marzo, aprile, maggio*

*l'estate*

*giugno, luglio, agosto*

*l'autunno*

*settembre, ottobre, novembre*

*l'inverno*

*dicembre, gennaio, febbraio*

## First, second, third . . .

| | |
|---|---|
| **il primo (m)/la prima (f)** | 1st |
| **il secondo/la seconda** | 2nd |
| **il terzo/la terza** | 3rd |
| **il quarto/la quarta** | 4th |
| **il quinto/la quinta** | 5th |
| **il sesto/la sesta** | 6th |
| **il settimo/la settima** | 7th |
| **l'ottavo/l'ottava** | 8th |
| **il nono/la nona** | 9th |
| **il decimo/la decima** | 10th |

Then drop the final "i" of the number and add **esimo/a**, e.g. **undici**: **undicesimo** (11th).

*Gennaio è il primo mese dell'anno.*

*Febbraio è il secondo mese dell'anno.*

*Dicembre è il dodicesimo mese dell'anno.*

Can you say where the rest of the months come in the year?

*Internet link:* a list of expressions for describing the weather in Italian. Click on "play other activities" for a choice of games that will help you learn the weather words. Go to **www.usborne-quicklinks.com** for a link to this site.

# What is the date?

Oggi è il tre maggio.

Quanti ne abbiamo oggi?

Oggi è il primo gennaio.

## Writing the date

Roma, 3 maggio 1987

The date is written 1, 2, 3 … and the month (which does not take a capital letter). For "the first", you write 1, but say **il primo**.

# When is your birthday?

Quand'è il tuo compleanno?

È il dieci novembre.

Il mio compleanno è il dodici febbraio.

Il compleanno di Simone è l'otto giugno.

# When are their birthdays?

The dates of the children's birthdays are below their pictures. Can you say in Italian when they are, e.g. **Il compleanno di Giulia è il due aprile**.

| Giulia | Massimo | Elena | Clara | Claudio | Enzo |
|--------|---------|-------|-------|---------|------|
|  |  |  |  |  |  |
| 2 aprile | 21 giugno | 18 ottobre | 31 agosto | 3 marzo | 7 settembre |

39

# Colours and numbers

**Internet link:** *solve a crossword puzzle about Italian numbers. Go to* **www.usborne-quicklinks.com** *for a link to this site.*

Colours are describing words, but only some of them change according to whether they are describing a masculine or feminine word.

## The colours

*rosso/a   blu   giallo/a   verde   arancione   rosa   nero/a   bianco/a   grigio/a   marrone*

## What colour is it?

Cover the picture above and see if you can say what colour everything is in the painting. You should know all the words you need.*

## Numbers

In Italian, you count the 30s to the 90s in the same way as 20-29. To count the 100s, you put the numbers 2 to 9 in front of 100. For the 1000s, you put the numbers 2 to 999 in front of 1000, but **mille** changes to **mila** (plural).

| | | | | | | | |
|---|---|---|---|---|---|---|---|
| 1 | uno | 11 | undici | 21 | ventuno | 40 | quaranta |
| 2 | due | 12 | dodici | 22 | ventidue | 50 | cinquanta |
| 3 | tre | 13 | tredici | 23 | ventitre | 60 | sessanta |
| 4 | quattro | 14 | quattordici | 24 | ventiquattro | 70 | settanta |
| 5 | cinque | 15 | quindici | 25 | venticinque | 80 | ottanta |
| 6 | sei | 16 | sedici | 26 | ventisei | 90 | novanta |
| 7 | sette | 17 | diciassette | 27 | ventisette | 100 | cento |
| 8 | otto | 18 | diciotto | 28 | ventotto | 200 | duecento |
| 9 | nove | 19 | diciannove | 29 | ventinove | 1000 | mille |
| 10 | dieci | 20 | venti | 30 | trenta | 2000 | duemila |

*"The sky" is **il cielo**.

# Pronunciation guide

*Internet link:* listen to the Italian alphabet. Go to **www.usborne-quicklinks.com** for a link to this site.

In Italian, many letters are pronounced differently from the way they are said in English. The best way to learn to speak Italian is to listen carefully to Italian people and copy what they say, but here are some general points to help you.

Below is a list of letters, with a guide to how to pronounce each one. For each Italian sound we have shown part of an English word which sounds like it. Read it out loud in a normal way to find out how to pronounce the Italian sound, then practise saying the examples beneath.

**a**  Like the "a" sound in "car", but shorter:
**Rom<u>a</u>, <u>a</u>mic<u>a</u>, l<u>a</u>, pizz<u>a</u>**

**e**  Like the "e" sound in "egg":
**<u>è</u>, <u>e</u>cco, t<u>e</u>tto, spagh<u>e</u>tti**

**i**  Like the sound "ee" in "keen", but a bit shorter:
**<u>i</u>tal<u>i</u>ano, n<u>i</u>do, <u>i</u>o, c<u>i</u>ttà, s<u>ì</u>**

**o**  Like the sound "o" in "odd":
**i<u>o</u>, tett<u>o</u>, babb<u>o</u>, am<u>o</u>**

**u**  Like the sound "oo" in "book":
**<u>u</u>va, c<u>u</u>cina, t<u>u</u>, <u>u</u>no**

**ce, ci**  "C" is soft before an "e" or "i" like the "ch" sound in "church":
**<u>ci</u>ao, uc<u>c</u>ello, cu<u>c</u>ina, mi pia<u>ce</u>**

**ca, co, cu**  Before an "a", "o", or "u", "c" is hard like in "cake":
**<u>c</u>asa, <u>c</u>osa, <u>c</u>oca-<u>c</u>ola, s<u>c</u>usi**

**che, chi**  Before "he" or "hi", "c" is hard like the "k" in "kettle":
**<u>chi</u>esa, <u>che</u> cosa, <u>chi</u>ami, <u>chi</u>**

**ge, gi**  "G" before an "e" or "i" is like the "j" in "jar":
**<u>ge</u>lato, man<u>gi</u>are, buon<u>gi</u>orno, <u>ge</u>nnaio**

**ga, go, gu, gr**  Before an "a", "o", "u", or "r", "g" is hard like the "g" in "game":
**ne<u>g</u>ozio, <u>gr</u>azie, <u>gu</u>ardare**

**ghe, ghi**  An "h" makes "g" hard before "e" or "i":
**spa<u>ghe</u>tti**

**gli**  Like the sound "li" in "million", with your tongue flat against the roof of your mouth:
**fami<u>gli</u>a, <u>gli</u>**

**gn**  Like the sound "ni" in "onion", with your tongue flat against the roof of your mouth:
**si<u>gn</u>ora, si<u>gn</u>ore, si<u>gn</u>orina**

**sce, sci**  Like the sound "sh" in "shut":
**pi<u>sci</u>na, pe<u>sce</u>**

**h**  "H" is never pronounced. "**io ho**" is pronounced "io o"

41

# Grammar

Grammar is like a set of rules about how you put words together and it is different for every language. You will find Italian easier if you learn some of its grammar, but don't worry if you don't understand all of it straightaway. Just read a little about it at a time. This is a summary of the grammar used in this book.

## Nouns

In Italian nouns are either masculine or feminine: (m) or (f). Most (m) nouns end in **o**. Most (f) nouns end in **a**. Some nouns end in **e** and are either (m) or (f). To make the plural, you usually change the last letter to **i** for (m) nouns and **e** for (f) nouns:

|     | singular | plural |
| --- | --- | --- |
| (m) | **albero** (tree) | **alberi** (trees) |
|     | **mobile** (cupboard) | **mobili** (cupboards) |
| (f) | **finestra** (window) | **finestre** (windows) |
|     | **televisione** | **televisioni** |

The Italian for "the" often tells you whether a noun is (m) or (f).

## il, lo la, l'

In the singular, "the" is

**il** or **lo** before (m) nouns (**il tetto**, **lo steccato**)
**la** before (f) nouns (**la finestra**)
**l'** before (m) and (f) nouns beginning with a vowel (**l'albero**, **l'insalata**).

## i, gli, le

In the plural "the" becomes

**i** for **il** nouns (**i tetti**)
**gli** for **lo** and (m) **l'** nouns (**gli steccati**, **gli alberi**)
**le** before **la** and (f) **l'** nouns (**le finestre**, **le insalate**).

A few (m) and (f) nouns have an accent on the last vowel. These don't change in the plural: **il caffè/i caffè**, **la città/le città**.

## al, allo, all', alla, ai, agli, alle

When **a** (at, to) is followed by **il**, they join and become **al**:

**Marco è al mercato**  Marco is at the market.

In the same way **a** + **lo** become **allo**:

**Il gatto è a fianco allo steccato**  the cat is next to the fence.

**a** + **la** become **alla**:

**Monica è alla stazione**  Monica is at the station.

**a** + **l'** become **all'**, **a** + **i** become **ai**, **a** + **gli** become **agli**, **a** + **le** become **alle**.

## del, dello, dell', della, dei, degli, delle

When **di** (of) is followed by **il**, they join and become **del**: **il prezzo del pane**  the price of bread.

In the same way **di** + **lo** become **dello**, **di** + **l'** become **dell'**, **di** + **la** become **della**, **di** + **i** become **dei**, **di** + **gli** become **degli**, **di** + **le** become **delle**.

**Del**, **dello** etc. also mean "some", "any":

**Lui mangia della carne**  he is eating some meat.

**Da** (from) + **il** become **dal**, **da** + **lo** become **dallo** etc.
**In** in) + **il** become **nel**, **in** + **lo** become **nello** etc.
**Su** (on) + **il** become **sul**, **su** + **lo** become **sullo** etc.

## un, uno, una

The word for "a/an" is **un** before **il** and masculine **l'** words, **uno** before **lo** words, **una** before **la** words and **un'** before feminine **l'** words:

| | |
| --- | --- |
| **un libro (m)** | a book |
| **uno strumento (m)** | an instrument |
| **una mela (f)** | an apple |
| **un'arancia (f)** | an orange |

## My, your

The word for "my" or "your" changes depending on whether the word that follows is (m), (f), singular or plural. In Italian you usually put "the" before "my" or "your":

| | |
| --- | --- |
| **il mio/il tuo libro** | my/your book |
| **la mia/la tua casa** | my/your house |
| **i miei/i tuoi fratelli** | my/your brothers |

## Adjectives

An adjective is a describing word. Italian adjectives change their endings depending on whether they are describing an (m) or (f), singular or plural word.

|  | singular | plural |
|---|---|---|
| (m) | **lui è alto** (he is tall) | **i nonni sono alti** (the grandparents are tall) |
| (f) | **lei è alta** (she is tall) | **le zie sono alte** (the aunts are tall) |

Some adjectives end in **e** in the singular, whether (m) or (f):

**Mio nonno è inglese**    my grandfather is English.
**Mia nonna è inglese**    my grandmother is English.

These always end in **i** in the plural, whether (m) or (f):

**Gli amici sono inglesi**    the friends are English.
**Le sorelle sono inglesi**    the sisters are English.

## Pronouns

When talking to one person, there are two words for "you" in Italian: **tu** and **lei**. You say **tu** to a friend and **lei** when you want to be polite or when you are talking to someone you don't know well.

Pronouns are often left out: **Mangio una mela** I eat an apple. Where in English you say "it is", in Italian you use the verb on its own: **è delizioso** it is delicious.

| singular | | plural | |
|---|---|---|---|
| **io** | I | **noi** | we |
| **tu** | you (a friend) | **voi** | you |
| **lei** | you (polite), she | **loro** | they |
| **lui** | he | | |

## Verbs

Italian verbs (doing words) change according to who is doing the action. Most of them follow regular patterns and have the same endings. The main type of verb used in this book ends in **are**, like **mangiare** (to eat). There are some verbs in this book which do not follow this pattern, e.g. **avere, essere** and **andare**. It is best to learn these as you go along.

| **mangiare** | to eat |
|---|---|
| **io mangio** | I eat |
| **tu mangi** | you eat (friend) |
| **lui/lei mangia** | he/she eats, you eat (polite) |
| **noi mangiamo** | we eat |
| **voi mangiate** | you eat (plural) |
| **loro mangiano** | they eat |

## Non

To make a verb negative in Italian, e.g. to say "I do not ...", "he does not ..." etc., you put **non** immediately before the verb:

**Io non suono il piano**  I do not play the piano.

## Reflexive verbs

These are verbs which always have a special pronoun in front of them. To say "I get up" in Italian, you say "I get myself up". The pronoun changes according to who is doing the action, but **mi** always goes with **io**, **ti** with **tu** etc.

| **alzarsi** | to get up |
|---|---|
| **io mi alzo** | I get up |
| **tu ti alzi** | you get up (friend) |
| **lui/lei si alza** | he/she gets up, you get up (polite) |
| **noi ci alziamo** | we get up |
| **voi vi alzate** | you get up (plural) |
| **loro si alzano** | they get up |

# Answers to puzzles

p.7

**What are they called?**
Lui si chiama Piero.
Lei si chiama Maria.
Loro si chiamano Paolo e Gianni.
Io mi chiamo . . . (your name).

**Who is who?**

Michele is talking to Gianni.
Anna is talking to Valeria.
Michele is next to the seal.
Gianni is talking to him.
Anna is in the bottom left-hand corner.
The man talking to Nicola is going home.

**Can you remember?**

Come ti chiami?
Io mi chiamo . . .
Questa è una mia amica. Si chiama Valeria.
Lui si chiama Daniele.

p.9

**Can you remember?**

un/il fiore, un/il gatto, un/l'albero, un/il
nido, un/l'uccello, un/il tetto, il sole, una/
la finestra, una/la macchina, un/il cane

p.11

**Who comes from where?**

Franz comes from Austria.
They are called Hari and Indira.
Lolita is Spanish.
Yes, Angus comes from Scotland.
Marie and Pierre come from France.
Yuri lives in Budapest.
Budapest is in Hungary.

**Can you remember?**

Da dove vieni?
Io vengo da . . .
Io parlo italiano.
Tu parli italiano?

p.13

**How old are they?**

Michele is 13.
Diana and Silvia are 15.
Giulio is 12.
Paola is 11.
Luca is 9.
Lisa is 5.

**How many brothers and sisters?**

A = Diana e Silvia. B = Luca. C =
Michele. D = Giulio. E = Paola.

p.17

**Where is everyone?**

Simone è in cucina.
Nonno è nella stanza da pranzo.
Nonna è nel soggiorno.
Mamma è nella stanza da letto.
Il fantasma è nella stanza di Isabella.
Isabella è al piano di sopra.
Piero è in bagno.

Nonno. Simone. Piero. Mamma.

Nella stanza da letto.
Nella stanza di Isabella.
Nella stanza da pranzo.
In bagno.
Nell'ingresso.

**Can you remember?**

Dove abiti?
Tu abiti in una casa o in un appartamento?
In campagna.
In città.
Io sono al piano di sopra.
Io sono in cucina.

p.19

**Where are they hiding?**

Il criceto è dentro il vaso.
Il gatto è dietro la televisione.
Il cane è dentro il mobile.

Il pappagallo è sopra lo scaffale.
Il serpente è sotto il divano.
La tartaruga è a fianco al telefono.

## p.21

### Who likes what?

1. Diego 2. Gianni 3. Nonno

## p.23

### Who is saying what?

"Ho fame."
"Buon appetito!"
"Prego, serviti."
"Mi puoi passare un bicchiere per favore?"
"Vuoi ancora patate fritte?"
"Sì grazie. Mi piacciono le patate fritte."
"No grazie. È abbastanza."
"È delizioso."

## p.25

### What are they doing?

A. Lui cucina. B. Lui nuota. C. Loro ballano.
D. Lei suona il violino. E. Lui dipinge.

## p.27

### Marco's day

1b, 2e, 3f, 4a, 5h, 6g, 7d, 8c.

### What time is it?

A   Sono le tre e cinque.
B   Sono le undici e cinque.
C   Sono le nove meno dieci.
D   Sono le quattro meno un quarto.
E   Sono le tre e venticinque.
F   Sono le sette e mezza.
G   Sono le tre.
H   Sono le quattro.
I   Sono le nove.
J   È l'una e mezza.
K   Sono le sette e cinque.
L   Sono le dieci e mezza.
M   Sono le sei.
N   Sono le tre e trentacinque.
O   Sono le due meno cinque.

## p.29

Venerdì sera vado a ballare con Diego.
Gioco a tennis lunedì, mercoledì e domenica.
Vado al cinema mercoledì sera.
Martedì.
Domenica gioco a tennis.
La festa è alle sette.

## p.33

Scusi, come si va al mercato?
Scusi, c'è un bar qui vicino?
È lontano?

Prenda la terza strada a sinistra, poi
diritto.

Prenda la terza a destra poi diritto. Il
mercato è sulla sinistra.
To the school.

## p.37

Vorrei quattro limoni, un chilo di banane
e un ananas, per favore.
Duecento Lire l'uno.
Duemila e cinquecento Lire al chilo.
Duemila Lire l'uno.
un ananas. le pesche. l'uva. un limone.

## p.39

Il compleanno di Giulia è il due aprile.
Il compleanno di Massimo è il ventuno
giugno.
Il compleanno di Elena è il diciotto ottobre.
Il compleanno di Clara è il trentuno agosto.
Il compleanno di Claudio è il tre marzo.
Il compleanno di Enzo è il sette settembre.

## p.40

La strada è grigia.
Il sole è giallo.
Il tetto è arancione.
Il cielo è blu.
I fiori sono rosa.
Il cane è marrone.
L'uccello è nero.
La macchina è rossa.
Gli alberi sono verdi.
La casa è bianca.

# Glossary

Adjectives and pronouns are shown in their masculine singular form. Irregular plurals of nouns are shown in brackets next to the letters "pl".

| | |
|---|---|
| a | at, to |
| a fianco a | next to |
| a piedi | on foot |
| abbastanza | enough, sufficient |
| abitare | to live |
| l'acqua (f) | water |
| l'aeroporto (m) | airport |
| affettuoso | friendly |
| agosto | August |
| l'albergo (m) | hotel |
| l'albergo della gioventù (m) | youth hostel |
| l'albero (m) | tree |
| gli alimentari | groceries, grocery shop |
| allora | then |
| alto | tall |
| altrettanto | the same to you (answer to "buon appetito") |
| altro | more, anything else, other |
| alzarsi | to get up |
| amare | to love |
| l'amburgher (m) | hamburger |
| l'amico/l'amica | friend (m/f) |
| l'ananas (m) (pl. gli ananas) | pineapple |
| anche | also, too |
| ancora | more |
| andare | to go |
| l'anno (m) | year |
| l'appartamento (m) | flat |
| aprile | April |
| l'arancia (f) | orange (fruit) |
| arancione (m/f) | orange (colour) |
| l'armadio (m) | wardrobe |
| arrivederci | Goodbye |
| ascoltare | to listen to |
| l'autunno (m) | autumn |
| l'Austria (f) | Austria |
| avere | to have |
| aver fame | to be hungry |
| | |
| il babbo | Dad |
| il bagno | bath, bathroom |
| ballare | to dance |
| la banana | banana |
| la banca | bank |
| il bar | café |
| basso | short (of height) |
| basta così? | is that all? |
| bene | well |
| bianco | white |
| il bicchiere | glass (for drinking) |
| biondo | blond |
| blu | blue |
| la buca delle lettere | post box |
| buon appetito | Enjoy your meal! |
| buonasera | Good Evening |
| buongiorno | Hello, Good Day |

| | |
|---|---|
| buono | good |
| il burro | butter |
| | |
| la cabina telefonica | phone box |
| il caffè | coffee |
| il calcio | football |
| la campagna | countryside |
| il campeggio | campsite |
| il cane | dog |
| la carne | meat |
| la cartolina | postcard |
| la casa | house |
| castano | chestnut (brown) |
| il castello | castle |
| c'è | there is |
| la cena | supper, evening meal |
| cercare | to look for |
| certo | certainly |
| che cosa? | what? |
| che ore sono? | what time is it? |
| che peccato! | what a pity! |
| chi? | who? |
| la chiesa | church |
| il chilo | kilo |
| ci vediamo | see you . . . |
| il cinema | cinema |
| ciao | Hello/Goodbye |
| la cioccolata | chocolate |
| la città | city, town |
| la coca-cola | coca-cola |
| la colazione | breakfast |
| come stai? | how are you? |
| come ti chiami? | what is your name? |
| il comignolo | chimney |
| il compleanno | birthday |
| comprare | to buy |
| continuare | to continue |
| il conto | bill |
| cosa? | what? |
| costare | to cost |
| il criceto | hamster |
| la crostata di frutta | fruit tart |
| la cucina | kitchen |
| cucinare | to cook |
| | |
| da | from |
| dare | to give |
| davanti a | in front of |
| delizioso | delicious |
| dentro | inside |
| desiderare | to wish |
| dicembre | December |
| dietro | behind |
| di fronte a | opposite |
| dipingere | to paint |
| di più | more |
| il divano | sofa |
| domani | tomorrow |
| la domenica | Sunday |
| dove | where |
| | |
| e | and |
| ecco | there is, here is |
| eccolo/a | there he, it/she, it is |
| essere | to be |
| l'estate (f) | summer |

| | | | |
|---|---|---|---|
| la famiglia | family | la madre | mother |
| la fame | hunger | maggio | May |
| il fantasma | ghost | magro | thin |
| fare | to do/make | male | badly, unwell |
| fare colazione | to have breakfast | mamma | Mum |
| fare la spesa | to go shopping (for food) | mangiare | to eat |
| la farmacia | chemist's | marrone | brown |
| febbraio | February | il martedì | Tuesday |
| la festa | party | marzo | March |
| la finestra | window | la mattina (or il mattino) | morning |
| fino a | as far as | la mela | apple |
| il fiore | flower | il mercato | market |
| il formaggio | cheese | il mercoledì | Wednesday |
| la Francia | France | il mese | month |
| il fratello | brother | la mezzanotte | midnight |
| la frutta | fruit | il mezzogiorno | midday |
| | | mezzo | half |
| il gabinetto | toilet | mi | me, myself |
| il garage (pl. i garage) | garage | mio | my, mine |
| il gatto | cat | mi piace | I like |
| la gazzosa | lemonade | il mobile | cupboard |
| il gelato | ice cream | il modellismo | model-building |
| i genitori | parents | molto | a lot, much, very |
| gennaio | January | il municipio | town hall |
| la Germania | Germany | la musica | music |
| giallo | yellow | | |
| giocare | to play | né | neither, nor |
| giovane (m/f) (pl. giovani) | young | il negozio | shop |
| il giovedì | Thursday | nero | black |
| girare | to turn | nessun(o)/a | not any (m/f) |
| giugno | June | il nido | nest |
| grasso | fat | niente | nothing |
| grazie | thank you | nient'altro? | anything else? |
| grigio | grey | no | no |
| guardare | to look | non . . . affatto | not at all |
| | | la nonna | grandmother |
| in | in | il nonno | grandfather |
| l'India (f) | India | novembre | November |
| l'Inghilterra (f) | England | nuotare | to swim |
| inglese | English | nuovo | new |
| l'inglese (m) | English language | | |
| l'ingresso (m) | entrance, hall | o | or |
| l'insalata (f) | salad | oggi | today |
| l'inverno (m) | winter | l'ospedale (m) | hospital |
| l'Italia (f) | Italy | ottobre | October |
| italiano | Italian | | |
| l'italiano (m) | Italian language | il padre | father |
| | | il pane | bread |
| là, lì | over there | il panettiere | baker |
| il latte | milk | il panificio | baker's |
| lavorare | to work | il panino | bread roll |
| lavorare a maglia | to knit | papà | Dad |
| leggere | to read | il pappagallo | parrot |
| il letto | bed | parlare | to speak |
| il limone | lemon | le patate fritte | chips |
| la Lira | Lira (Italian money) | passare | to pass |
| il litro | litre | la pesca | peach |
| lontano | far | il pesce | fish |
| luglio | July | il piano di sopra | upstairs |
| il lunedì | Monday | la pianta | plant |
| | | il pianoforte | piano |
| ma | but | la piazza | square |
| il macellaio | butcher | la piscina | swimming pool |
| la macelleria | butcher's | la pizza | pizza |
| la macchina | car | un poco | a little |

| | | | |
|---|---|---|---|
| poi | then, after | la stanza | room |
| la poltrona | armchair | la stanza da letto | bedroom |
| il pomeriggio | afternoon | la stanza da pranzo | dining room |
| il pomodoro | tomato | stare bene | to be well |
| la porta | door | stasera | tonight, this evening |
| la posta | post office | la stazione | station |
| il pranzo | lunch | la stazione di servizio | petrol station |
| prego | not at all (answer to "grazie") | lo steccato | fence |
| preferire | to prefer | la strada | road |
| prendere | to take | lo strumento musicale | musical instrument |
| presto | soon | su | on, over |
| la primavera | spring | sulla destra/sinistra | on the right/left |
| primo | first | il succo | juice |
| pronto | ready | suonare | to play music |
| proprio | just | il supermercato | supermarket |
| il prosciutto | ham | | |
| | | il tappeto | carpet |
| qualcosa | something | la tartaruga | tortoise |
| quando? | when? | la tavola | table |
| quanti? | how many? | il tè | tea |
| quanti ne abbiamo? | what is the date? | tedesco | German |
| quanto? | how much? | il tedesco | German language |
| quarto | fourth, quarter | il telefono | telephone |
| quasi | almost | la televisione | television |
| questo, quello | this, that | il tempo libero | spare time |
| qui | here | la tenda | curtain |
| | | il tennis | tennis |
| il riso | rice | terzo | third |
| in riva al mare | by the sea | il tetto | roof |
| rosa | pink | ti | yourself |
| la rosa | rose | la torta | cake |
| rosso | red | tra | between |
| | | trovare | to find |
| il sabato | Saturday | tuo | your, yours |
| la salsiccia | sausage | | |
| lo scaffale | shelf | l'uccello (m) | bird |
| la Scozia | Scotland | l'ufficio del turismo (m) | tourist office |
| la scuola | school | un, una, uno | a, an |
| scusi | excuse me | l'Ungheria (f) | Hungary |
| secondo | second | l'uno/l'una (m/f) | each |
| la sera | evening | l'uovo (m) (pl. le uova, f) | egg |
| il serpente | snake | l'uva (f) | grapes |
| serviti | help yourself | | |
| settembre | September | va bene | all is well, O.K. |
| sì | yes | il vaso | vase |
| signora | madam, Mrs. | vecchio | old |
| signore | Sir, Mr. | il venerdì | Friday |
| signorina | Miss | venire | to come |
| il sole | sun | verde | green |
| solo | only, alone | la verdura | vegetables |
| il soggiorno | living room | verso | towards |
| sopra | above, on | la via | street |
| soprattutto | above all | vicino | near |
| la sorella | sister | il violino | violin |
| sotto | under | volere | to want |
| gli spaghetti (pl) | spaghetti | | |
| la Spagna | Spain | la zia | aunt |
| lo sport (pl. gli sport) | sport | lo zio | uncle |

First published in 1987 by Usborne Publishing Ltd, 83-85 Saffron Hill, London EC1N 8RT, England. www.usborne.com